Sound Effects for Streaming

Essential Guide for Content Creators

Ethan Prescott

© Copyright 2024 Ethan Prescott

All rights reserved

Ethan Prescott

Sound Effects for Streaming

© Copyright 2024 Ethan Prescott

All rights reserved

Copyrights Notice

No part of this book may be reproduced in any form or by any electronic or mechanical means, including information storage and retrieval systems, without written permission from the author.

Recording of this publication is strictly prohibited and any storage of this document is not allowed unless with written permission from the publisher.

All rights reserved. Respective authors own all copyrights not held by the publisher.

Pictures used for the cover are of the respective owners, granted to the Author in a Royalty-Free license.

All trademarks, service marks, product names, and the characteristics of any names mentioned in this book are considered the property of their respective owners and are used only for reference. No endorsement is implied when we use one of these terms.

Ethan Prescott

Limitation of Liability - Disclaimer

Please be aware that the content of this book is derived from the author's personal experiences and research from various information sources. The information provided is intended solely for educational and creative purposes, and no warranties of any kind, express or implied, are made.

Readers should understand that the author is not providing professional sound engineering or audio production advice. Prior to implementing any techniques or strategies presented in this book, it is highly recommended to seek guidance from a qualified sound designer, audio engineer, or other relevant industry expert, especially when working on complex media projects.

Nothing in this book is intended to replace professional consultation, sound engineering best practices, or common sense. The examples and methods described may not be suitable for every individual's specific needs or circumstances. The reader assumes all risks associated with the use of the information in this book and is responsible for their own actions and results.

While the information herein is presented as truthful and consistent to the best of the author's knowledge, any liability arising from oversight, inattention, or the misapplication of the policies, processes, or directions contained within, is the sole responsibility of the reader.

By reading this book, the reader agrees that under no circumstances shall the author be held accountable for any direct or indirect losses incurred as a result of using the information within this document. This includes, but is not limited to, errors, omissions, or inaccuracies.

Table Of Contents:

Introduction 9

Chapter 1: Fundamentals of Sound Effects for Streaming 13

1.1 Understanding the Psychological Impact of Sound Effects 13

1.2 Sound Design Techniques for Streaming 17

1.3 Essential Tools for Sound Effect Production 20

1.4 Legal and Ethical Aspects of Sound Effects in Streaming 24

Chapter 2: Practical Applications of Sound Effects 29

2.1 Sound Effects for Different Streaming Genres 29

2.2 Advanced Synchronization Techniques 33

2.3 Customizing Sound Effects for Your Brand 37

2.4 Optimizing Sound Effects for Different Platforms 41

Chapter 3: Innovation and the Future of Sound Effects in Streaming 45

3.1 Emerging Technologies in Sound Design for Streaming ... 45

3.2 Creating Interactive Experiences Through Sound Effects 49

3.3 Data Analysis and Optimization of Sound Effects 52

3.4 Collaborations and Networking in the World of Sound Effects 56

Conclusion 61

Stay Connected and Explore More! 65

Introduction

Welcome to the fascinating and rapidly evolving world of sound effects for streaming. In an era dominated by online audiovisual content, the auditory component plays a crucial role in capturing the audience's attention and creating memorable experiences. Sound effects, far from being mere embellishments, are a fundamental element in enhancing live broadcasts, enriching podcasts, and making videos more engaging.

The importance of sound effects in the streaming landscape cannot be underestimated. They serve as a powerful narrative tool, capable of evoking emotions, building atmospheres, and reinforcing the message you wish to convey. A well-crafted jingle can become a channel's trademark, while a strategically placed sound effect can highlight a key moment or elicit an immediate reaction from viewers.

In the competitive context of streaming platforms, where the fight for attention is fierce, skillful use of sound effects can make the difference between content that goes unnoticed and content that leaves a mark.

This book aims to be a comprehensive and essential guide for all content creators who wish to master the art of sound effects in streaming. Whether you are just starting your journey or are an established professional seeking new inspiration, you will find a wealth of knowledge, techniques, and strategies in these pages to elevate the audio quality of your productions.

Throughout the chapters, we will explore the psychological foundations that make sound effects so effective in capturing and maintaining audience attention. We will analyze sound design techniques specific to streaming, considering the peculiarities of this medium and the expectations of modern viewers. I will guide you through the selection of essential tools, both software and hardware, needed to create a functional and efficient workspace.

I will also address legal and ethical aspects, providing you with the necessary knowledge to navigate the complex world of copyright and licenses, ensuring you can use sound effects responsibly and professionally. We will then move on to practical applications, exploring how to adapt sound effects to different streaming genres, from gaming to talk shows, from podcasts to live events.

I will reveal advanced techniques for synchronization and customization, allowing you to create a unique library of sound effects that reflects your channel's identity. We will tackle technical challenges related to optimizing sound effects for various platforms, ensuring that your work shines on Twitch, YouTube, Facebook Gaming, and beyond.

Looking to the future, we will explore emerging technologies in the field of sound design for streaming, from the potential of binaural audio to the use of artificial intelligence in generating sound effects. I will show you how to create interactive experiences through sound, engaging your audience in innovative and memorable ways.

To make the most of this guide, I encourage you to approach it with an open mind and a spirit of experimentation. Each chapter is designed to build your skills progressively, starting from fundamental concepts to more advanced techniques. Do not hesitate to put into practice what you learn: true mastery is achieved through hands-on experience and continuous experimentation.

I invite you to consider this book not just as a technical manual, but as a source of inspiration. As you delve into the various topics, let your creativity run wild. Try new combinations of effects, dare to experiment with unusual sounds, and push the boundaries of conventional sound design for streaming.

Remember that the world of sound effects is constantly evolving, just like the streaming world itself. What you find in these pages is a solid starting point, but the real journey begins when you close the book and start applying this knowledge in your daily work.

Therefore, I encourage you to stay curious, continue learning, and adapt to new trends and technologies that will emerge. Join online communities of sound designers and content creators, participate in workshops and conferences, and challenge yourself with ambitious projects. Only then will you remain at the forefront of this dynamic and competitive field?

Whether you are a gaming enthusiast, a podcast host, a live event streamer, or a content creator in any other domain, the tools and knowledge you acquire through this guide will enable you to elevate the audio quality of your productions to new levels of excellence. Prepare to embark on an exciting and transformative sonic journey that will redefine how you think about and use sound effects in your streaming.

Chapter 1: Fundamentals of Sound Effects for Streaming

"The sound of a story can be as crucial as the visuals." - Walter Murch, film editor and sound designer

Sound, in its purest essence, is a primal force capable of touching the deepest chords of the human soul. In the sector of streaming, this power manifests through sound effects—subtle yet extraordinarily effective tools for shaping the viewer's experience. As Walter Murch, a renowned film editor and sound designer, notes, "The sound of a story can be as crucial as the visuals." This insight, originally intended for film, is equally relevant to streaming, capturing the essence of what we will explore in this chapter: the fundamentals of sound effects and their psychological impact on the audience.

1.1 Understanding the Psychological Impact of Sound Effects

To fully understand the power of sound effects, we must first delve into the fascinating world of psychoacoustics, the science that studies human perception of sound. Sound frequencies, invisible to the eye but tangible to the ear and body, can profoundly influence our emotional state. Deep basses can evoke a sense of gravity or threat, while high frequencies can generate tension or excitement.

This knowledge is crucial for those who wish to skillfully manipulate their audience's emotions through streaming.

Consider, for example, the effect of low frequencies. A constant rumble at 20 Hz, barely perceptible to the human ear, can induce a feeling of unease or even fear. It is no coincidence that this trick is widely used in films to create an atmosphere of latent tension. In the context of streaming, judicious use of these frequencies can enhance viewer engagement, keeping them literally on the edge of their seats during an enthralling narrative or a crucial moment in gameplay.

On the other hand, higher frequencies have the power to stimulate and activate. A sharp, sudden sound can instantly capture attention, making it ideal for signaling important events during a stream. Imagine an alert sound for a significant donation or the entrance of a special guest: a well-designed sound effect in this frequency range can electrify the audience and create a memorable moment.

But the art of sound effects goes far beyond mere frequency manipulation. One of the most powerful techniques available to content creators is using sound to create cycles of tension and release. This dynamic, fundamental in music and cinematography, can be applied with great effectiveness in streaming as well.

Imagine a gaming streamer approaching a crucial moment in an intense game. A gradual increase in the volume of a suspenseful sound effect, perhaps accompanied by a slight rise in frequency, can build palpable tension. When the jumpscare finally occurs, a sudden change in the soundscape—perhaps a sharp scream or a dissonant chord—provides the cathartic release of that tension.

This cycle of build-up and release not only keeps viewers hooked but also creates a shared emotional experience that strengthens the bond between the streamer and their audience.

Immersion is another crucial aspect of the streaming experience that can be significantly enhanced through the skillful use of sound effects. In this context, immersion refers to the ability to make the viewer feel like an integral part of the environment or narrative presented in the stream. Sound effects play a fundamental role in creating this sense of presence.

Consider a streamer conducting ASMR (Autonomous Sensory Meridian Response) sessions. In this case, the entire content revolves around creating an immersive auditory experience. Using binaural microphones and advanced recording techniques allows for creating a three-dimensional soundscape that envelops the listener. Sound effects, ranging from the rustling of turning pages to the delicate tinkling of crystals, are designed to stimulate specific sensory responses, creating a deeply immersive and relaxing experience.

However, immersion through sound effects is not limited to niche genres like ASMR. In a live role-playing stream, for instance, adding subtle environmental effects—the crackling of a campfire, the whistling of the wind in a cave, and the background noise of a crowded tavern—can transport both players and viewers into the fantastical world of the narrative. These seemingly minor sound details build an acoustic fabric that supports and enriches the narrative experience.

The effectiveness of sound effects in enhancing immersion largely depends on their authenticity and strategic placement. A poorly synchronized or unrealistic sound effect can break the illusion and jarringly pull the viewer out of the experience. Conversely, well-crafted and skillfully integrated sound effects can blur the boundary between the real world and the stream, creating an engaging and memorable experience.

It is important to note that the psychological impact of sound effects can vary significantly from person to person. Cultural factors, personal experiences, and even physiological differences can influence how an individual perceives and responds to certain sounds. This variability underscores the importance of knowing your audience and being willing to experiment and continuously refine the use of sound effects.

Furthermore, the effectiveness of sound effects is not only in their presence but also in their absence. Silence, used strategically, can be as powerful a tool as any elaborate sound effect. A sudden moment of silence in an otherwise sound-rich stream can create a dramatic impact, drawing the viewer's attention and setting the stage for what follows.

In summary, understanding the psychological impact of sound effects is a fundamental skill for any streaming content creator. From subtly manipulating emotions through frequencies, to creating cycles of tension and release, to building deeply immersive experiences, sound effects offer a vast arsenal of tools to elevate the quality and impact of your content. Mastering this art requires not only technical skills but also a deep understanding of human psychology and a keen sensitivity to the nuances of the auditory experience.

1.2 Sound Design Techniques for Streaming

In the vast landscape of streaming, where countless content creators compete for audience attention, the ability to stand out is essential. Sound design offers a unique opportunity to create a distinctive auditory identity that leaves a lasting impression on viewers.

Creating a unique sound signature for your channel is akin to designing a visual logo: it should be immediately recognizable, memorable, and consistent with the overall identity of your brand. This sound signature can manifest in various ways: an opening jingle, a recurring sound effect, or even a particular way of handling audio that permeates the entire production.

To develop this sound signature, start by reflecting on the essence of your channel. What emotions do you want to evoke? What is the general tone of your content? Once these elements are defined, you can begin experimenting with different sounds and compositions. Consider using instruments or sounds that reflect the theme of your channel. For instance, a retro gaming streamer might incorporate 8-bit sounds into their signature, while a nature channel might use field recordings of natural environments.

Consistency is crucial in creating an effective sound signature. Once key elements are established, ensure they are used consistently throughout your content. This does not mean your sound signature must remain static; rather, it can evolve but should retain a recognizable core that viewers can immediately associate with your channel.

Balancing sound effects and the main content is a delicate art requiring sensitivity and practice. Sound effects should enhance the viewer's experience without ever overpowering or distracting from the central message of your stream. This balance varies significantly depending on the type of content you are producing.

In an informational podcast, for example, sound effects should be used sparingly, primarily as emphasis points or transitions between topics. On the other hand, in a gaming stream, sound effects can play a more prominent role, highlighting moments of action or victory. The goal is always to enhance the overall experience, not to compete with the main content.

An effective approach is to create a sound hierarchy for your stream. At the top of this hierarchy will always be the main content—whether it's your voice, the gameplay, or any other central element of your stream. Sound effects should be layered beneath this primary level, creating a supporting sound fabric that enriches without overwhelming.

Attention to mixing is fundamental in this process. Use equalization to ensure that sound effects occupy different frequencies than the main content, thus avoiding audio conflicts. Compression can help control the volume peaks of sound effects, keeping them consistently below the level of the main content.

Layering techniques represent a powerful tool for creating sound depth in your stream. Layering involves stacking multiple sounds or effects to create a rich and complex soundscape. This technique can transform flat, one-dimensional audio into an engaging and immersive experience.

Effective layering starts with a clear understanding of the three-dimensional sound space. Think of your audio in terms of foreground, midground, and background. The foreground might contain direct and immediate sound effects, such as donation notifications or specific reactions. The midground could include environmental elements that support the theme of your stream, while the background might be filled with subtle atmospheric sounds that create a sense of space and depth.

An advanced layering technique is the use of "ghost sounds"—nearly imperceptible effects that add texture and richness to the audio without being consciously noticed by the viewer. These might include low-volume environmental noises, subtle reverbs, or even subsonic frequencies that are felt more than heard.

Automation can be a powerful ally in layering. By using audio production software, you can program subtle changes in volume, panning, and effects of various sound layers throughout the stream. This can create a dynamic soundscape that evolves in response to the events of the stream, keeping the auditory experience fresh and engaging.

It's important to remember that while layering is powerful, it requires a measured approach. Excessive sound layers can lead to confusing and tiring audio. Every added element should have a specific purpose and contribute significantly to the overall experience.

Experiment with different sound combinations, playing with the relative volume and stereo placement of each layer. Listen carefully to how the different elements interact with each other and with the main content of your stream. Don't be afraid to remove elements if the mix becomes too dense; sometimes, less is more when creating an effective soundscape.

Finally, consider the importance of contrast in your sound design. Alternating moments of rich sound with periods of relative simplicity can create a dynamic rhythm in your stream, maintaining listener interest and avoiding auditory fatigue.

1.3 Essential Tools for Sound Effect Production

In the world of streaming, the quality of sound effects can make the difference between a mediocre and an extraordinary experience. To achieve excellence in this field, it's crucial to have the right software and hardware tools and create a work environment that fosters creativity and efficiency. This section will explore the essential tools for sound effect production, providing an overview of the most suitable audio editing software for streamers, a guide to necessary hardware, and tips for setting up an ergonomic workspace for sound design.

In the vast array of audio editing software, choosing the right program might seem daunting for a beginner streamer. However, with a clear understanding of your needs and the desired level of complexity, finding the ideal solution is possible. For those new to sound design, Audacity is an excellent option. This open-source software provides a comprehensive suite of basic audio editing tools, is free, and boasts an active and supportive user community. Its intuitive interface makes it accessible to beginners while offering enough functionality to create quality sound effects.

For those seeking a higher level of control and flexibility, Reaper stands out as an excellent choice. This professional Digital Audio Workstation (DAW) offers a wide range of features at an affordable price. Its highly customizable nature makes it ideal for streamers who wish to create a workflow tailored to their specific needs. Reaper excels in managing complex projects and provides a broad range of compatible plugins, allowing you to expand your sound design capabilities as you gain experience.

At the top of the pyramid are software programs like Pro Tools and Adobe Audition. These programs, though they come with a steeper learning curve and higher cost, offer the highest quality in terms of audio and creative possibilities. Pro Tools is the industry standard in music and film, providing unmatched precision and sound quality. Adobe Audition, on the other hand, integrates seamlessly with other Creative Cloud software, making it an excellent choice for streamers who also work with video and graphics.

Turning to hardware, the microphone is the first and most crucial element in the audio production chain. For streaming and sound effect creation, a high-quality USB condenser microphone such as the Blue Yeti or the Rode NT-USB is an excellent starting point. These microphones offer excellent audio quality, plug-and-play setup, and the versatility needed to record both voice and environmental sound effects.

For those looking to go further, investing in a professional XLR microphone like the Shure SM7B, paired with a quality audio interface, can significantly elevate recording quality. An audio interface like the Focusrite Scarlett 2i2 not only allows for the use of professional XLR microphones but also offers high-quality preamps and the ability to record multiple audio sources simultaneously.

Dedicated audio interfaces play a crucial role in improving the overall quality of your system's audio. Models such as the Native Instruments Komplete Audio 6 or the Universal Audio Apollo Twin offer superior digital-to-analog conversion, reduce latency, and provide additional audio inputs and outputs. This allows you to easily integrate musical instruments, hardware synthesizers, or other audio devices into your streaming setup.

MIDI controllers are another valuable tool for streamers who want precise, tactile control over their sound effects. Devices like the AKAI MPK Mini or the Novation Launchpad offer pressure-sensitive pads and assignable knobs that can be mapped to various audio parameters in your software. This enables you to trigger sound effects, adjust real-time parameters, and add a live performance element to your streams.

Creating an ergonomic workspace for sound design is essential for maintaining productivity and preventing long-term health issues. Start with an adjustable-height desk that allows you to alternate between sitting and standing during long work sessions. An ergonomic chair with proper lumbar support is crucial for maintaining good posture and reducing fatigue during extended editing sessions.

Position your monitor(s) at eye level to avoid neck strain, and consider using an adjustable monitor stand for added flexibility. For audio, invest in a pair of high-quality studio monitors placed correctly to create an ideal "listening triangle." This will allow you to accurately perceive your mix and make informed decisions about your sound design.

Lighting plays a crucial role in an ergonomic workspace. Opt for a combination of ambient lighting and an adjustable desk lamp to reduce eye strain. Natural light is ideal, but if it's not available, consider using full-spectrum lamps that mimic daylight.

Workspace organization is equally important. Use cable organizers and management systems to keep your area tidy and free of tangles. This not only improves the aesthetic of your workspace but also reduces the risk of accidents and makes equipment maintenance easier.

Don't underestimate the importance of room acoustics. Even the best equipment can be compromised by a poor acoustic environment. Consider adding acoustic panels or diffusers to treat sound reflections and improve listening accuracy. Strategically place bass traps in the corners of the room to manage problematic low frequencies.

Remember that your workspace should evolve with you. As you gain experience and refine your craft, you may find the need for new tools or a different setup. Be open to experimenting and adjusting your configuration to find what works best for you. With the right tools and an optimized work environment, you'll be prepared to create professional-quality sound effects that elevate your streams to new levels of excellence.

1.4 Legal and Ethical Aspects of Sound Effects in Streaming

In the world of streaming, creativity and originality are crucial, making it important to be well-informed about the various legal and ethical aspects of using sound effects. Understanding copyright and licensing for sound effects is essential for any streamer who wants to operate professionally and legally.

Copyright protects creative works, including sound effects, from the moment they are created. This means that unauthorized use of a copyrighted sound effect can lead to serious legal consequences, including lawsuits and claims for damages.

Licenses are the mechanism through which content creators can legally use copyrighted sound effects. There are various types of licenses, each with its specifics and restrictions. Royalty-free licenses, for example, allow unlimited use of a sound effect after a one-time payment. These are particularly popular among streamers for their simplicity and cost-effectiveness. However, it is crucial to carefully read the terms of the license, as there may be limitations on use in certain contexts or on the distribution of the final content.

Creative Commons licenses offer an interesting alternative, allowing creators to specify exactly how their works can be used. Some CC licenses permit commercial use and modification of the original work, while others are more restrictive. It is essential to understand the nuances of these licenses to avoid unintentional violations.

For streamers using platforms like Twitch or YouTube, it is important to familiarize yourself with each platform's specific policies regarding the use of copyrighted audio content. These platforms often have automated systems to detect unauthorized use of protected content, which can lead to video demonetization or, in more severe cases, channel suspension.

Given this complex landscape, many streamers face the dilemma of whether to create original sound effects or use pre-existing libraries. Creating original sound effects offers several advantages. First, it ensures the uniqueness of your content, allowing you to stand out in a saturated market. Additionally, it eliminates any concerns related to copyright, as you own 100% of the created material.

However, producing high-quality sound effects requires technical skills, specific equipment, and, most importantly, time. For many streamers, especially those who are just starting out or have limited resources, this can be a significant barrier. In these cases, using pre-existing libraries can be a practical and effective solution.

Sound effect libraries offer a wide range of professional sounds ready for use. Many of these libraries come with clear and easily understandable licenses, reducing the risk of unintentional copyright violations. Moreover, using well-curated libraries can significantly enhance the overall audio quality of your stream, especially for those without experience in sound effect creation.

The choice between original sound effects and pre-existing libraries doesn't necessarily have to be binary. Many successful streamers adopt a hybrid approach, creating some key custom effects that define their channel's identity while drawing from libraries for more generic or background effects.

Beyond legal aspects, the use of sound effects in streaming raises important ethical questions, especially when they are used to influence viewers. Sound effects have significant power in shaping audience emotions and perceptions, and with this power comes responsibility.

A fundamental ethical consideration is transparency. Should streamers be clear about using sound effects to emphasize or dramatize certain moments? Or is the illusion an integral part of the entertainment experience? There is no universally correct answer to these questions, but each content creator needs to reflect on these implications and make informed decisions.

Using sound effects to manipulate viewers' emotions, while a common practice in the entertainment industry, requires careful consideration in the streaming context. For example, the use of subliminal sounds or anxiety-inducing frequencies might be considered unethical, especially if the audience includes minors or vulnerable individuals.

Another ethical aspect to consider is authenticity. In an era where genuineness is increasingly valued by audiences, excessive or artificial use of sound effects might be perceived as deceptive. Finding a balance between enhancing the experience through sound effects and maintaining perceived authenticity is a challenge every streamer must face.

The issue of accessibility is another important ethical consideration. Sound effects can significantly improve the experience for many viewers, but they might also create barriers for users with hearing disabilities. Streamers should consider how to make their content accessible to everyone, such as by providing textual descriptions of significant sound effects or offering options to disable certain types of effects.

Finally, it is important to reflect on the cumulative impact of sound effects on viewers' well-being. In an age where many people spend hours watching streams, prolonged exposure to certain types of sound effects could have long-term effects on mental health and viewer well-being. Streamers have the responsibility to consider not only the immediate impact of their sound effects but also the potential long-term consequences of their use.

Applying these legal and ethical aspects requires a combination of knowledge, reflection, and sensitivity. Successful streamers are those who not only master the technical aspects of sound effects but also understand the broader implications of their use. By maintaining an ethical and legally aware approach, it is possible to harness the power of sound effects to create engaging and memorable content while respecting the rights of other creators and the well-being of your audience.

Ethan Prescott

Chapter 2: Practical Applications of Sound Effects

"Sound is 50% of the cinematic experience." - George Lucas

The renowned director George Lucas once stated, "Sound is 50% of the cinematic experience." This maxim, though born in the context of cinema, applies with equal force to the world of streaming. In this chapter, we will explore the practical applications of sound effects across different streaming genres, demonstrating how sound can transform an ordinary experience into something extraordinary and memorable.

2.1 Sound Effects for Different Streaming Genres

In the field of gaming streaming, sound effects play a crucial role in creating immersive atmospheres and providing essential sound feedback. A skilled game streamer understands that audio is much more than a mere accompaniment to visual gameplay; it is a fundamental element that can elevate the entire experience. For example, in a fantasy adventure game, the strategic use of evocative ambient sounds, such as birds chirping in a forest or the crackling of a fire in a campsite, can greatly enhance the sense of exploration and immersion for viewers.

Sound feedback in gaming streaming goes beyond the sounds within the game itself. Experienced streamers integrate custom sound effects to highlight key moments in the gameplay. A distinctive sound for epic kills, a jingle for viewer donations, or a humorous sound effect for major failures can become trademarks of the streamer, creating a cohesive and recognizable auditory experience. These sound elements not only enrich the stream but also help build a community around the channel, with viewers learning to anticipate and appreciate these characteristic sound touches.

Moving to the world of talk shows and streaming podcasts, sound effects assume a different but equally crucial role. In this context, the primary goal is to structure and pace the content, guiding listeners' attention through the narrative or discussion. Jingles, for instance, are much more than catchy melodies. A well-designed jingle acts as a Pavlovian signal for viewers, announcing the start of the show and mentally preparing the audience for the experience about to begin. Similarly, shorter jingles or "stingers" can be used to signal transitions between different segments of the show, helping to maintain a consistent flow and avoid abrupt interruptions.

Sound transitions in a talk show or podcast are the audio equivalent of film editing cuts. They can be subtle—such as a gentle fade-out/fade-in—or more pronounced, like a distinctive sound effect that clearly separates different sections of the program. The art lies in finding the right balance: too frequent or intrusive transitions can be distracting, while well-calibrated transitions enhance the rhythm and overall structure of the show.

Sound Effects for Streaming

The concept of the "sound bed" is particularly relevant for talk shows and podcasts. A sound bed is a constant background sound that creates an atmosphere and fills any silences. It can range from a subtle white noise to specially composed ambient music. Choosing the right sound bed can significantly influence the perceived tone of the show: an energetic sound bed can keep the energy high during a lively discussion, while a softer background can create an intimate atmosphere for deeper conversations.

Live event streaming presents a unique set of challenges and opportunities in the field of sound effects. Unlike gaming or pre-recorded talk shows, live events require real-time sound management, with little to no margin for error. Managing ambient sound is crucial in this context. Whether it's a concert, a sports event, or a conference, capturing the atmosphere of the surrounding environment is essential for conveying to viewers at home the feeling of "being there."

However, managing ambient sound goes beyond mere capture. It involves careful balancing between the event sound and the streamer's commentary, ensuring that neither element overwhelms the other. Techniques such as "ducking"—where the background audio volume is automatically lowered when the streamer speaks—can be crucial for maintaining commentary clarity without losing the event's atmosphere.

Implementing real-time sound effects during live event streaming requires a mix of preparation and improvisation. An experienced streamer will have a library of pre-loaded sound effects, ready to be used at the right moment. These can range from simple "swooshes" for camera transitions to more elaborate effects to highlight key moments of the event. The key is in judicious use: sound effects should enhance the event experience, not distract from it.

An often-overlooked aspect of live event streaming is managing silence. Many events have moments of pause or transition that, if left completely silent, can seem dead or technically problematic for viewers at home. The subtle addition of a light sound bed or ambient effects can keep the stream's flow and keep viewers engaged even during these quiet moments.

Technological advancements are opening new frontiers in the application of sound effects to live event streaming. Technologies such as binaural audio or object-based audio are enabling increasingly immersive sound experiences, allowing viewers to feel truly at the center of the action. Although still in the adoption phase, these technologies promise to revolutionize how we perceive and interact with streamed events.

Regardless of the streaming genre, effective application of sound effects requires a deep understanding not only of audio techniques but also of listening psychology. When used skillfully, sound effects become a subliminal language that communicates directly with viewers' emotions and senses. Whether it's intensifying the adrenaline of a gaming session, guiding attention through a complex discussion in a podcast, or transporting viewers to the heart of a live event, sound effects are the tool that transforms streaming from a simple flow of information into an engaging and memorable experience.

2.2 Advanced Synchronization Techniques

In live broadcasts, precise synchronization of acoustic elements can make the difference between a mediocre and an extraordinary experience. Advanced synchronization techniques allow broadcasters to create a dynamic and responsive auditory environment that seamlessly integrates with visual and interactive content.

The use of MIDI triggers for automated sound effects represents a significant leap in efficiency and precision in audio production for live broadcasts. MIDI triggers are essentially digital signals that can be used to activate or modify acoustic elements in real-time. This approach allows presenters to pre-program a wide range of sounds that can be instantly triggered in response to specific events during the live broadcast.

To implement this technique, it is first necessary to configure a MIDI interface that acts as a bridge between the broadcasting software and the audio software. Many modern Digital Audio Workstations (DAWs) natively support MIDI input, making it relatively easy to integrate this system. Once the connection is established, the host can assign specific MIDI messages to particular acoustic elements or audio parameters.

A practical example might be the use of MIDI triggers in a gaming broadcast. The presenter could set up a MIDI trigger to activate a victory sound every time a level is completed or a boss is defeated. This not only adds a level of professionalism to the broadcast but also frees the presenter from the need to manually trigger these sounds, allowing them to focus on gameplay and interaction with the audience.

MIDI automation can be taken further, allowing dynamic modifications of acoustic elements based on various parameters. For example, the volume or pitch of a sound could be modulated based on the intensity of the action on screen, creating an auditory landscape that organically adapts to the visual content.

Creating macros for complex sound compositions represents the next step in the evolution of sound design for live broadcasts. In this context, a macro is a pre-programmed sequence of audio actions that can be triggered with a single command. These macros enable presenters to create elaborate, multi-layered sounds that would be impossible to perform manually in real-time.

To create effective macros, it is essential to have a clear vision of the desired effect and a thorough understanding of the audio software used. Many modern DAWs offer scripting or automation features that can be leveraged to create complex macros. For example, a macro might combine a fade-in of background music, activation of a reverb effect on the host's voice, and triggering of a custom jingle, all with the press of a single key.

Macros can be particularly useful in broadcasting situations that require rapid transitions between different audio "scenes." In a live talk show, for example, a macro could manage the entire sound transition between segments, including fading out current music, activating a transition effect, and fading in new background music.

The true power of macros emerges when combined with real-time input. Using MIDI controllers or custom keyboards, presenters can create a physical interface for sound control, allowing intuitive and tactile manipulation of the broadcast's auditory landscape.

Synchronizing acoustic elements with visual components and chatbots represents the cutting edge of synchronization techniques for live broadcasts. This multi-dimensional integration creates a cohesive and immersive experience that engages all of the viewer's senses.

In terms of synchronization with visual elements, the possibilities are virtually limitless. In a gaming broadcast, for example, sounds could be synchronized not only with the player's actions but also with graphical overlays appearing on the screen. An animation of a new channel subscription could be accompanied by a custom sound that perfectly syncs with the graphical movement.

The use of real-time video compositing software, such as OBS (Open Broadcaster Software), allows for even more precise synchronization between audio and video. Through the use of plugins and custom scripts, it is possible to create triggers that simultaneously activate visual and auditory effects, creating multimedia moments that capture the audience's attention.

Integrating acoustic elements with chatbots adds an additional layer of interactivity to the broadcast. Chatbots, automated programs that interact with viewers in the live chat, can be configured to trigger sounds in response to specific commands or events. This not only enriches the viewer experience but also creates a sense of direct participation in the broadcast.

For example, a chatbot could be programmed to trigger a celebratory sound when a viewer reaches a certain number of loyalty points or makes a significant donation. Alternatively, in a role-playing game broadcast, viewers could use specific chat commands to activate ambient sounds, thus actively contributing to the atmosphere of the game.

The key to effective synchronization with chatbots lies in creating a robust system that can handle multiple simultaneous inputs without overwhelming the broadcast audio. This requires careful planning and implementation of priority and cooldown systems to avoid audio chaos.

Implementing these advanced synchronization techniques requires a combination of technical skills, creativity, and a deep understanding of the live broadcast medium. Presenters who master these techniques can create rich and engaging audiovisual experiences that stand out in an increasingly crowded landscape.

However, it is important to remember that technology is only a tool. The true art lies in knowing when and how to use these sounds to enhance the overall broadcast experience rather than distract from it. Perfect synchronization of acoustic elements should be almost imperceptible, working at a subconscious level to guide the emotions and attention of the viewers.

As technology continues to evolve, we can expect to see new and innovative synchronization techniques emerge. The integration of technologies such as augmented reality and spatial audio promises to elevate live broadcast experiences to new levels of immersion. Presenters who stay at the forefront of these developments will be well-positioned to create content that not only entertains but truly transports viewers into rich and engaging auditory worlds.

2.3 Customizing Sound Effects for Your Brand

Given the competitiveness of the streaming industry, customizing sound effects is a crucial element for standing out and creating a unique and memorable brand identity. This process goes well beyond simply selecting pre-made sounds; it requires a strategic and creative approach that aligns every auditory element with the essence of your channel.

Creating a custom sound effects library forms the foundation of this strategy. This acoustic archive becomes the sound palette from which to draw to paint the auditory identity of your stream. Start by identifying key moments in your content that would benefit from a distinctive sound accent. These might include the stream's introduction, transitions between segments, notifications for new followers or donations, or recurring moments specific to your format.

Once these moments are identified, the next step is producing the sound effects. This phase offers a unique opportunity to infuse your personality and the tone of your channel into each sound. If you have sound design skills, you might choose to create sounds from scratch using synthesizers or field recordings. Otherwise, collaborating with a professional sound designer can be a valuable investment to achieve high-quality effects that perfectly align with your vision.

Consistency is crucial in building your library. Consider developing a "sound signature"—a recurring acoustic element that, like a visual logo, becomes immediately associated with your brand. This could be a short musical motif, a distinctive sound effect, or even a particular audio processing technique consistently applied to your sounds.

Sound morphing techniques offer an innovative approach to expand and adapt your sound effects library. Sound morphing is essentially the art of gradually transforming one sound into another, creating a smooth transition, or generating entirely new sounds in the process. This technique not only allows for greater variety from your existing library but also helps maintain overall sound consistency.

To implement sound morphing, start by selecting two sound effects from your library that you want to blend. Use specialized audio morphing software or advanced features of many modern Digital Audio Workstations (DAWs) to create a series of intermediate sounds. This process can generate surprising and unique effects that retain recognizable elements of the original sounds while being completely new.

Sound morphing can be particularly effective for creating variations of a recurring sound effect. For example, you might have a base sound for new follower notifications but use morphing to create slightly different versions for different donation levels or subscription milestones. This approach maintains a base consistency while offering variety and progression.

In addition to morphing, consider using audio processing techniques to further adapt and personalize existing effects. Pitch manipulation, adding effects like reverb or delay, or applying filters can radically transform a sound while still maintaining a connection to the original. Experiment with these techniques to create a sound palette that is both cohesive and versatile.

The strategic use of sound effects to reinforce channel identity is the ultimate goal of this customization process. Sound effects should not merely be embellishments but integral elements that communicate and reinforce your brand's message and atmosphere.

Start by clearly defining your channel's identity. What are the values, tone, and atmosphere you wish to communicate? A gaming channel focused on high-energy action games will require a very different sound palette compared to a channel dedicated to philosophical discussions or art tutorials. Once this identity is established, every sound effect should be evaluated based on how effectively it supports and amplifies it.

Consider using sound "leitmotifs" for recurring characters or segments of your live broadcast. Just like in a musical score, these recurring sound themes can create a sense of cohesion and familiarity for your audience. For example, in a true crime podcast, you might have a distinctive sound effect that always introduces the evidence analysis segment, creating a Pavlovian anticipation in your audience.

Consistency in the use of sound effects is important for reinforcing channel identity. Establish clear guidelines on when and how to use specific effects. This consistency helps your audience navigate the flow of content and strengthens the association between these sounds and your brand.

Do not underestimate the emotional power of sound effects in shaping your channel's perception. Warm and welcoming sounds can contribute to creating a sense of community and intimacy, while more energetic and dynamic effects can emphasize excitement and action. Carefully align the emotional tone of your sound effects with the sentiment you wish to evoke in your audience.

The evolution of your sound identity should be an ongoing process. As your channel grows and evolves, so should your sound effects adapt and refine. Be open to feedback from your audience and do not be afraid to iterate and constantly improve your sound library.

Also, consider how your sound effects translate across different platforms and devices. A sound that works perfectly on desktop speakers may lose its impact on mobile devices. Test your effects on a variety of playback systems to ensure they retain their effectiveness and identity in different listening contexts.

Remember, authenticity is key. Your custom sound effects should be a natural extension of your personality and streaming style. Avoid forcing sounds or styles that do not authentically align with your brand simply because they are trendy. The audience perceives and appreciates authenticity, and sound effects that genuinely reflect your identity will help build a deeper and more lasting connection with your viewers.

2.4 Optimizing Sound Effects for Different Platforms

In the diverse streaming ecosystem, the ability to optimize sound effects for various platforms stands out as a key skill for content creators aiming for excellence. Each platform, whether it's Twitch, YouTube, or Facebook Gaming, has its own technical and cultural peculiarities that directly impact the effectiveness and perception of sound effects. Mastering the art of adapting your acoustic arsenal to these different environments can make the difference between a mediocre audio experience and one that captures and holds the audience's attention.

Twitch, with its emphasis on real-time interaction, requires an approach to sound effects that prioritizes responsiveness and immediacy. Alerts for new followers, subscriptions, and donations need to be clear and distinguishable but short enough not to interrupt the stream flow. Given the wide range of donation volumes on Twitch, it's wise to implement a scalable sound effects system where the intensity or complexity of the sound increases proportionally with the donation amount. This not only adds a gamification element to the donation experience but also helps manage audience expectations.

YouTube, on the other hand, with its mix of live and on-demand content, requires a more versatile approach. Sound effects must work effectively both during live broadcasts and in edited videos. This dual requirement underscores the importance of creating effects that maintain their integrity and impact even after the additional compression applied during YouTube's upload and encoding process. Additionally, given the longer and more structured nature of many YouTube content pieces, there is room for more elaborate and narrative sound effects, which can be used to mark different sections of a video or create moments of emotional climax.

Facebook Gaming, although a relatively new platform in the live-streaming world, presents distinctive challenges. The platform tends to favor a more informal and socially connected viewing experience, implying that sound effects must be designed to quickly grab attention without being intrusive. Since many Facebook users might discover your content while scrolling through their feeds, it's crucial that your sound effects are immediately engaging but not disruptive to an audience potentially unfamiliar with live gaming conventions.

Technical considerations play a fundamental role in optimizing sound effects for these different platforms. Audio compression, in particular, is an aspect that requires meticulous attention. Each platform applies its compression algorithms to the audio stream, which can significantly alter the quality and impact of your sound effects. To counteract this, it is advisable to apply pre-compression to your effects, using settings that anticipate and mitigate the artifacts introduced by the platform's compression. This process requires experimentation and iteration but can result in sound effects that retain their integrity and power through various stages of transmission and playback.

Volume normalization is another crucial technical aspect. Since viewers can quickly switch from one stream to another, your sound effects must be well balanced not only within your stream but also relative to the platform's average levels. Use LUFS (Loudness Units relative to Full Scale) measurement tools to ensure your sound effects adhere to the platform's loudness standards, providing a consistent listening experience for your audience.

Choosing the appropriate audio format might seem like a minor detail, but it has significant implications for transmission quality and efficiency. While uncompressed formats like WAV offer the highest quality, their bandwidth weight can cause buffering or latency issues, especially on less stable connections. Formats like AAC or Opus offer a good compromise between quality and efficiency, maintaining high audio fidelity with significantly reduced file sizes.

Creating presets for different platforms and streaming situations represents a time investment that can yield enormous benefits in terms of efficiency and consistency. These presets should go beyond simple equalization and compression settings, also including configurations for audio routing, level management, and effect automation.

For Twitch, for example, you might create a preset that emphasizes responsiveness, with short and punchy sound effects, aggressive compression to maximize impact, and quick automation to handle real-time alerts. The YouTube preset might favor a broader dynamic range, with more elaborate sound effects and softer compression that preserves audio depth for on-demand viewing.

Different live-streaming scenarios require distinct sound approaches. A preset for high-energy gameplay sessions might emphasize energetic sound effects and compression that maintain clarity even in high audio intensity moments. Conversely, a preset for talk shows or more relaxed discussions might prioritize more delicate handling of sound effects, with smooth transitions and more space for the human voice.

Effective implementation of these presets requires a deep understanding not only of each platform's technical features but also of audience expectations and behaviors on them. Closely monitor engagement metrics and gather direct feedback from your viewers to continually refine these presets, ensuring they stay in tune with evolving platform dynamics and audience preferences.

An often-overlooked aspect of sound effects optimization is considering the different listening conditions of your audience. An experienced streamer will create sound effects that maintain their effectiveness whether played through high-end audio systems or simple smartphone speakers. This requires a sound design approach focused on clarity and emotional impact rather than subtle audio nuances that might be lost in less-than-ideal listening conditions.

Ultimately, consider that optimizing sound effects is not a static process but an ongoing evolution. Platforms regularly update their algorithms and technical specifications, and content consumption trends are constantly shifting. Stay updated on the latest audio best practices for each platform and do not hesitate to experiment with new approaches. Adaptability and a willingness to innovate in your sound design will be key to keeping your content fresh and engaging in the dynamic world of streaming.

Chapter 3: Innovation and the Future of Sound Effects in Streaming

"The future belongs to those who believe in the beauty of their dreams." — *Eleanor Roosevelt*

The streaming landscape is continually evolving, and with it, the technologies that shape the auditory experience. As Eleanor Roosevelt reminds us, "The future belongs to those who believe in the beauty of their dreams." In this chapter, we will explore the cutting-edge frontiers of sound design for streaming, where technological innovation merges with human creativity to create extraordinary auditory experiences.

3.1 Emerging Technologies in Sound Design for Streaming

One of the most promising technologies in sound design for streaming is binaural audio. This recording and playback technique aims to faithfully replicate the human auditory experience, creating a three-dimensional spatial illusion through standard stereo headphones. Binaural audio takes advantage of the subtle differences in how sound reaches each ear, allowing listeners to perceive the direction and distance of sound sources with remarkable precision.

For online presenters, implementing binaural audio opens up a range of creative possibilities. Imagine a tense gaming experience where the footsteps of an antagonist seem to come from behind the viewer or a virtual talk show where each guest's voice appears distinctly positioned in space. This technology not only enhances engagement but can also improve audio clarity in complex scenarios, enabling the audience to focus on specific sound sources in a rich acoustic environment.

However, adopting binaural audio in web broadcasts requires specific technical considerations. Digital hosts will need to invest in specialized recording equipment, such as binaural microphones or acoustic mannequins, and familiarize themselves with mixing techniques that preserve the spatial effect. It will also be crucial to educate the audience about the importance of using headphones to fully enjoy this immersive experience.

Another exciting frontier in sound design for live streaming is the use of artificial intelligence (AI) for generating soundscapes. AI is revolutionizing many aspects of audio production, and its potential in the context of web broadcasts is vast and largely unexplored.

AI systems can analyze the visual content of a live broadcast in real-time and automatically generate appropriate soundscapes. This could translate to a dynamic and reactive audio environment for video games, where the soundscape adapts instantly to player actions and on-screen events. For live content presenters, AI could suggest or apply relevant sound environments based on the context of the discussion or the overall atmosphere of the show.

In addition to reactive generation, AI can be used to create customized soundscape collections. By feeding the system examples of the desired acoustic style, online hosts could generate an endless array of unique atmospheres that perfectly align with their channel's identity. This not only saves time in searching for and manually creating environments but also opens the door to entirely new and unexpected sound qualities.

However, integrating AI into sound design also raises ethical and creative issues. Hosts will need to balance the efficiency and innovation offered by AI with the desire to maintain a personal and authentic touch. Additionally, it will be essential to be aware of the legal complexities related to copyright for AI-generated content.

Augmented audio reality (AAR) represents perhaps the boldest and most unexplored frontier in the future of sound design for online broadcasts. This technology promises to seamlessly blend the digital world with the physical one, creating sound experiences that interact with the viewer's real environment.

Imagine a scenario where the soundscapes of a web broadcast are not confined to headphones or speakers but seem to come from specific points in the viewer's room. A dragon's roar might seem to emerge from the window, while the clinking of coins might seemingly come from under the couch. This fusion of virtual and physical reality could take engagement to previously unimaginable levels.

For online hosts, AAR offers the opportunity to create unique interactive experiences. A virtual tour could guide viewers through their homes, with sounds and narratives anchored to specific objects and places in their physical space. Fitness presenters could use AAR to create a motivating sound environment that adapts to each viewer's individual workout space.

However, implementing AAR in web broadcasts presents significant challenges. The technology requires specialized devices capable of mapping the user's environment and accurately placing sounds in three-dimensional space. The variety of home setups and devices used by viewers makes creating a consistent experience for everyone complex.

Moreover, digital hosts will need to develop new skills to effectively leverage this technology. Designing AAR experiences requires a deep understanding not only of sound design but also of psychoacoustics and human-computer interaction. There will be a need to completely rethink the approach to storytelling and audience engagement in this new immersive context.

Despite these challenges, the potential of AAR to revolutionize online broadcasts is undeniable. As the technology matures and becomes more accessible, we can expect to see entirely new forms of interactive entertainment emerge based on web streaming.

In summary, binaural audio, artificial intelligence, and augmented audio reality represent just the tip of the iceberg of innovations shaping the future of sound design in online broadcasting. These technologies promise to radically transform how we create, consume, and interact with online audio content. For visionaries in webcasting willing to embrace these new frontiers, unlimited possibilities await to create unique, engaging, and unforgettable sound experiences.

3.2 Creating Interactive Experiences Through Sound Effects

In the dynamic world of online broadcasting, interactivity has become key to capturing and maintaining audience attention. Ambient sounds, far from being mere embellishments, are transforming into powerful tools for creating engaging and participatory experiences.

One of the most exciting trends in this field is the integration of donation systems with customized acoustic triggers. This fusion of financial support and auditory gratification is redefining how viewers contribute and feel like an integral part of the live stream. Imagine a scenario where every donation not only supports the broadcaster but also activates a unique and memorable sound experience.

The most innovative presenters are creating true "acoustic menus" linked to donations. A modest contribution might trigger a brief, fun jingle, while more substantial donations could unleash elaborate sound sequences that momentarily interrupt the broadcast for a shared celebration. Some content creators are pushing this concept even further, allowing donors to customize their sound effects or unlock increasingly rare and desirable sounds as their support accumulates over time.

This practice not only incentivizes donations but also creates a sense of community and immediate recognition. Regular viewers learn to recognize the sounds associated with various community members, turning each donation into a moment of social connection. However, it is crucial to carefully balance the frequency and intensity of these sound elements to avoid overwhelming the viewing experience or excessively distracting from the main content of the broadcast.

Another exciting frontier in the interactive use of ambient sounds is the development of acoustic mini-games for audience engagement. These games, seamlessly integrated into the live stream, use audio as the main mechanic, offering a new level of participation for viewers.

An innovative example might be a "sound hunt" game, where viewers must quickly identify a specific sound element hidden within the audio mix of the broadcast. The first to recognize and report it in the chat could win a prize or special recognition. This not only keeps the audience attentive and engaged but also adds an element of suspense and friendly competition to the viewing experience.

Gaming presenters might implement acoustic challenges related to gameplay. For example, in a survival game, viewers could be invited to count the number of shots or explosions during an intense sequence, with prizes for those who guess the exact number. This dual focus—on the game and sound counting—creates a richer and more engaging viewing experience.

For broadcasters of educational or informational content, acoustic mini-games can become powerful teaching tools. A sound quiz could test viewers' knowledge on various topics, from music to nature, using audio clips as questions. This approach not only makes learning more interactive and fun but also leverages the mnemonic power of audio to reinforce information retention.

Creating interactive soundscapes driven by audience actions represents perhaps the most advanced and promising frontier in this field. This technique transforms the entire acoustic environment of the broadcast into a living, responsive entity that breathes and evolves based on the collective actions of the audience.

Imagine a virtual exploration stream where the soundscape changes dynamically based on decisions made by viewers through a real-time voting system. If the majority chooses to explore a rainforest, the audio gradually fills with exotic bird calls, raindrops on leaves, and distant roars of hidden predators. Conversely, if they opt for an underwater adventure, the soundscape transforms into a world of bubbles, distant echoes, and the mysterious songs of whales.

This technique can also be applied in surprising ways in less obvious contexts. An artistic content creator might develop a collaborative "sound canvas," where each viewer can add an acoustic element to an evolving composition. As the visual artwork takes shape on the screen, the soundscape enriches and complicates, reflecting the community's creative choices.

For music presenters, interactive soundscapes offer revolutionary possibilities. Imagine a live composition session where viewers can vote in real-time to influence elements such as tempo, key, or even the instruments used. The result is a unique and unrepeatable performance, co-created by the broadcaster and their audience.

Implementing these interactive soundscapes requires careful planning and robust technical infrastructure. Presenters must set up a vast library of ambient sounds and smooth transitions, as well as develop robust systems for interpreting and reacting quickly to audience inputs. Additionally, maintaining a delicate balance between the creative freedom offered to viewers and the overall coherence of the audio experience is essential.

These innovative applications of interactive ambient sounds are redefining the boundaries between creator and audience, transforming online broadcasts from a predominantly passive medium to a deeply participatory experience. As these techniques evolve and refine, we can expect to see entirely new forms of storytelling and entertainment emerge, where sound plays a central role in weaving meaningful connections between presenters and viewers.

3.3 Data Analysis and Optimization of Sound Effects

In the dynamic world of live online broadcasting, where competition is increasingly fierce, refining acoustic components through meticulous data analysis is emerging as an unexplored and crucial area for digital content creators. This fusion of sound art and analytical science offers web broadcasters a range of powerful tools to perfect their audio productions, enhance audience engagement, and create increasingly captivating and tailored auditory landscapes.

The use of analytical technologies to evaluate the impact of acoustic elements is the first fundamental step in this refinement process. Cutting-edge analytics platforms enable creators to monitor a wide range of audio-related metrics. These tools can track parameters such as view duration, viewer retention rates, and engagement peaks about specific sounds or auditory sequences.

For example, a creator might discover that introducing a particular jingle significantly increases the average view duration of the broadcast. Alternatively, they might notice that certain sound elements correlate with an increase in chat activity or a rise in social media shares. These insights allow broadcasters to identify which acoustic components resonate most with their audience and which may need revision or replacement.

Moreover, data analysis can reveal more subtle patterns in the interaction between audio and viewer behavior. A creator might find, for instance, that certain sounds are particularly effective in retaining new viewers during the critical first minutes of a live stream, or that specific ambient soundscapes correlate with longer viewing sessions during certain time slots.

A/B testing, a technique borrowed from digital marketing, is becoming an indispensable tool for optimizing the effectiveness of acoustic components in web broadcasts. This approach involves creating two or more versions of an audio element and presenting them to different groups of viewers to determine which version performs better according to predefined metrics.

For example, a creator might experiment with different variants of a donation notification sound. Version A could be a short melodic jingle, while Version B might be a more elaborate sound element thematically tied to the content of the broadcast. By distributing these variants to representative samples of their audience and analyzing the related engagement metrics, the broadcaster can scientifically determine which version elicits the most positive response.

A/B testing can be applied to various aspects of sound design, from the volume and duration of sounds to their frequency and contextual placement within the broadcast. This iterative process of experimentation and analysis allows creators to continuously refine their soundscape, creating a more optimized and engaging audio experience for their specific audience.

Dynamic adaptation of acoustic components based on real-time feedback represents the pinnacle of this fusion between data analysis and sound design. This advanced technique uses machine learning algorithms to constantly monitor audience reactions and adjust the broadcast audio in real-time to maximize engagement.

Imagine a scenario where the system detects a drop in audience attention during a gaming session. The algorithm might respond by subtly increasing the intensity of game sounds or introducing an element of tension in the ambient soundscape to reignite viewers' interest. Similarly, if real-time analysis indicates that a particular sound element is generating a particularly positive response in the chat, the system might slightly increase the frequency of that sound's use or introduce variations on that theme.

This adaptive approach can also extend to personalizing the audio experience for individual viewers or audience segments. Using historical data and individual preferences, the system could tailor the audio mix to optimize each viewer's listening experience. For instance, it could emphasize certain sounds for viewers who have shown a preference for them in the past or adjust the balance between voice and acoustic components based on individual listening habits.

Implementing these dynamic adaptation systems requires sophisticated technological infrastructure and a deep understanding of both sound design and data analysis. Broadcasters must invest in platforms capable of processing and analyzing large volumes of data in real-time, as well as developing sufficiently extensive and flexible sound libraries to enable smooth and contextually appropriate adaptations.

Furthermore, it is essential to balance data-driven optimization with artistic integrity and overall audio experience coherence. Too aggressive or frequent adaptation could be disorienting for viewers or compromise the overall atmosphere of the broadcast. Creators must therefore establish clear parameters for dynamic adaptation, ensuring that real-time changes remain subtle and in harmony with the overall tone of the content.

The ethics of data use is another crucial consideration in this field. Broadcasters must be transparent with their audience regarding the collection and use of data for audio optimization, ensuring compliance with privacy regulations and obtaining appropriate consent from viewers.

Despite these challenges, data analysis and optimization of acoustic components offer digital content creators extraordinary potential to elevate the quality and effectiveness of their audio content. This convergence of artistic creativity and analytical rigor is opening new frontiers in sound design for web broadcasts, allowing creators to forge deeper and more meaningful audio connections with their audience.

3.4 Collaborations and Networking in the World of Sound Effects

In the ever-changing ecosystem of streaming, networking and collaborations are foundational pillars for innovation and professional growth in the field of sound effects. This constantly evolving sector thrives on the exchange of ideas, sharing of knowledge, and synergy among diverse talents. In this context, building a vibrant community of sound designers dedicated to streaming emerges as an urgent necessity and an extraordinary opportunity.

The formation of such a community often starts organically through online forums, social media groups, or specialized platforms. However, to maximize its effectiveness, a structured approach is essential. Organizing regular webinars, constructive critique sessions, and virtual workshops can transform a simple aggregation of professionals into a true incubator of innovation. These events not only promote the exchange of techniques and best practices but also create a sense of belonging and mutual support, which is crucial in a field often characterized by individual and remote work.

An active community of streaming sound designers can also serve as a bridge between content creators and sound professionals, facilitating collaborations that enhance the overall quality of productions. Imagine a platform where streamers can post their specific sound design needs and professionals can offer their expertise, creating a dynamic marketplace of talent and opportunities.

Collaboration possibilities in the world of streaming sound effects extend well beyond the boundaries of the sound designer community. The intersection with the music world provides particularly fertile ground for creative partnerships. Musicians and sound artists, with their deep understanding of composition and musical emotion, can bring a new dimension to sound design for streaming.

For example, collaborating with a composer could result in the creation of custom musical themes that seamlessly integrate with the stream's sound effects, creating a cohesive and memorable sonic identity. Similarly, a field recording artist might provide a library of unique ambient sounds, capable of transporting viewers to never-before-explored sonic worlds.

These collaborations not only enrich the final product but also offer valuable opportunities for mutual learning. A sound designer might gain new perspectives on frequency manipulation from a music producer, while a musician might discover new ways to think about sound structure through the lens of streaming sound design.

To facilitate these collaborations, professional "speed dating" events could be organized, where sound designers and musicians have the opportunity to meet, exchange ideas, and potentially bring innovative projects to life. Online platforms could serve as showcases for portfolios and demos, allowing professionals from different backgrounds to discover and appreciate each other's work.

Another powerful vehicle for innovation and networking in the world of streaming sound effects is hackathons and sound design contests. These events, which can take place both in person and online, offer a unique arena where creativity, technical skill, and collaborative spirit converge in a crucible of innovation.

A sound design hackathon for streaming might, for example, challenge participants to create a complete suite of sound effects for a new streaming genre within just 48 hours. This kind of time pressure not only stimulates creativity but also encourages rapid prototyping and quick iteration—skills essential in the fast-paced world of streaming.

Contests, on the other hand, offer the opportunity to tackle more specific and targeted challenges. A competition might ask participants to create a unique sonic identity for an emerging web broadcast platform or to develop innovative sound effects to enhance stream accessibility for users with hearing impairments.

Participation in these events offers benefits that go beyond the chance to win prizes. They are valuable opportunities for receiving feedback from industry experts, building a diverse portfolio, and, most importantly, forging connections with other passionate and talented professionals.

To maximize the impact of hackathons and contests, it is crucial to involve industry sponsors and partners. Leading streaming platforms could provide access to their APIs to facilitate the integration of new sound effects. Audio hardware manufacturers might supply cutting-edge equipment for participants. This not only enriches the experience for competitors but also creates an ecosystem where innovation can flourish and be quickly adopted by the industry.

Documenting and sharing the results of these events is equally important. Creating an online repository of projects, ideas, and prototypes born during hackathons and contests can serve as a source of inspiration and a starting point for future innovations. Follow-up webinars where winners share their creative processes and lessons learned can transform these one-off events into ongoing learning opportunities for the entire community.

In the rapidly evolving landscape of sound effects for online streaming, isolation is the enemy of progress. Building a vibrant community, fostering interdisciplinary collaborations, and actively participating in competitive and collaborative events are more than just networking strategies—they are the engines driving innovation and excellence in this field. Through these channels, streaming sound design professionals not only expand their skills and opportunities but also collectively contribute to shaping the sonic future of the medium.

Ethan Prescott

Conclusion

Throughout the discussion of acoustic suggestions for live broadcasting, we have explored a vast array of concepts, techniques, and strategies that define this rapidly evolving art. At this point, it is crucial to reflect on the journey undertaken and look to the future with eyes full of possibilities and creative ambition.

Reviewing the chapters of this book, it is clear that sound textures are not mere adornments but essential elements capable of radically transforming the live broadcasting experience. We have discovered the psychological power of sound, its ability to evoke emotions, create atmospheres, and establish deep connections with the audience. Understanding these mechanisms provides a solid foundation upon which to build effective and engaging sound strategies.

The sound design techniques explored offer a versatile toolkit for creating rich and immersive soundscapes. From crafting a unique sonic signature that defines a channel's identity to achieving a delicate balance between acoustic suggestions and the main content, and through sophisticated layering techniques, every aspect contributes to shaping a memorable auditory experience. Mastery of these tools opens the door to endless creative possibilities, allowing each live broadcast to be elevated to a true sonic art form.

Ethan Prescott

The importance of tools and technologies cannot be underestimated. The careful selection of hardware and software, combined with a deep understanding of their capabilities, constitutes the technical foundation upon which the creative structure of sound design for live broadcasting is built. Awareness of ongoing innovations in this field, from binaural audio to artificial intelligence applied to sound generation, sets the stage for staying at the forefront of a constantly evolving industry.

However, the true essence of this book goes beyond the mere transmission of technical knowledge. Its deeper purpose is to ignite the spark of experimentation and innovation. The techniques and concepts presented are not immutable dogmas but starting points for creative exploration. Every broadcaster, and every sound designer, has the potential to push beyond known boundaries, discovering new ways to use sound to engage, move, and amaze their audience.

Encouraging innovation translates into a call to dare, challenge conventions, and think outside the box. Experiment with unexpected sound combinations, explore new modes of sonic interaction with your audience and dare to create acoustic textures that have never been heard before. Remember that every major innovation in sound design has originated from an act of creative boldness and a willingness to traverse uncharted paths.

In this spirit of continuous evolution and learning, it is important to stay connected with the broader community of professionals and enthusiasts in sound design for live broadcasting. Online resources are an inexhaustible mine of knowledge, inspiration, and support.

Specialized forums, social media groups, dedicated YouTube channels, and industry podcasts offer ongoing opportunities for updates and discussion.

Among the most valuable resources are online communities dedicated to sound design for live broadcasting. These platforms serve as meeting points for professionals at all levels, from novices to veteran experts. Here, you can share your creations, receive constructive feedback, participate in creative challenges, and stay updated on the latest industry trends and innovations. Interaction with peers from around the world not only broadens your creative horizons but also offers valuable networking and collaboration opportunities.

Do not underestimate the educational value of webinars and specialized online courses. Many leading professionals in the field of sound design for live broadcasting offer masterclasses and virtual workshops, allowing you to learn directly from the best. These events not only enrich your technical skill set but also provide valuable insights into industry practices and future directions.

Conferences and industry events, whether virtual or in person, represent another invaluable resource for your professional development. These gatherings offer the opportunity to attend cutting-edge presentations, participate in hands-on workshops, and, most importantly, establish personal connections with other industry professionals. Do not hesitate to actively participate by proposing your presentations or workshops: sharing your experiences and knowledge not only contributes to the growth of the community but also strengthens your position as an authoritative voice in the field.

Remember that learning in the world of sound design for live broadcasting is an ongoing and dynamic process. Technologies evolve, new platforms emerge, and audience preferences change. In this context, curiosity and the willingness to learn are your most valuable allies. Cultivate the habit of regularly exploring new tools, techniques, and approaches. Challenge yourself to master new software each month or to create a completely original acoustic suggestion each week.

Finally, do not forget the importance of staying connected with the world beyond sound design. Drawing inspiration from other art forms, from music to cinema, from visual arts to literature, can greatly enrich your creative approach. Similarly, being attentive to broader cultural and social trends will allow you to create sound textures that deeply resonate with your audience, capturing the zeitgeist of the moment.

The study of sound effects for streaming that you have undertaken with this book is only the beginning. A universe of sonic possibilities awaits exploration. With the knowledge acquired, the encouragement of innovation, and the resources at your disposal, you are now equipped to leave your unique mark on the soundscape of live broadcasting.

May your journey be filled with discoveries, successes, and, above all, extraordinary sounds that captivate the imagination and touch the hearts of your audience!

Stay Connected and Explore More!

Thank you for reading "Sound Effects for Streaming". If you found this book helpful and want to continue exploring the world of sound design, there are several ways to stay connected and get even more value:

- **Leave a Review:** Your feedback is incredibly important! If you enjoyed this book, please take a moment to leave a review on Amazon. Your review helps other readers find this book and lets me know how I can continue to improve.

- **Follow Me on YouTube**: For a deeper dive into sound effects, subscribe to my YouTube channel "Elite Sound Effects". I regularly upload videos that showcase creative sound effects and offer insights into the latest trends in audio.

- **Get in Touch:** Have questions, feedback, or collaboration opportunities? Feel free to email me at powermedia.nx@gmail.com. I'd love to hear from you and assist with any inquiries you might have.

- **Explore More Books:** Check out my other books available on Amazon. I cover various aspects of sound design and related topics that can further enhance your skills and knowledge.

- **Discover Useful Journals and Planners:** Don't miss out on my collection of journals and planners designed to help you organize your creative projects and stay on track. Find them on Amazon.

Thank you for your support, and I look forward to connecting with you through these channels!

Sound Effects for Streaming

© Copyright 2024 Ethan Prescott

All rights reserved

www.ingramcontent.com/pod-product-compliance
Lightning Source LLC
Chambersburg PA
CBHW030048230526
45471CB00003B/988